FOREWORD

This is a season of miracles and wonders; a time to celebrate the glorious impossible of God's magnificent gift of grace.

Celebrate FAITH as God speaks His living Word into the darkness and awakens the world to His promise of grace.

Celebrate HOPE as God's glory bursts into the darkness like a thousand stars of light.

Celebrate PEACE as God speaks to a young girl who embraces the Divine with gentle obedience.

Celebrate LOVE as we gather to gaze into a humble manger.
See heaven's King choose a cradle of compassion rather than a throne of power.

Celebrate JOY as the Judean hillsides echo with the voices of angels proclaiming good tidings to simple shepherds.

Celebrate LIGHT as a sacred star shines silver promise on golden sand.
Walk with the dreamers and seekers to a place of devotion and worship.

Celebrate LIFE and walk the path of service.
Humble your hearts with thanksgiving, worship, and prayer.
Bow, bend, and become.

Let the darkness see and believe.

Let the shadows surrender to light.

Let the miracle begin!

Come celebrate Jesus!

Know the wonder of grace!

INVITATION TO A MIRACLE
Overture

Arranged by
JOSEPH M. MARTIN (BMI)

Based on tunes:
**WEXFORD CAROL,
KOMMET IHR HIRTEN,
THE HOLLY AND THE IVY,
TEMPUS ADEST FLORIDUM,
BRANLE DE L'OFFICIEL,**
and **MENDELSSOHN**

* Tune: WEXFORD CAROL, traditional Irish melody

INVITATION TO A MIRACLE - SAB

INVITATION
— TO A —
Miracle

By Joseph M. Martin
Orchestrations by Brant Adams and Stan Pethel

(1) This symbol indicates a track number on the StudioTrax CD
(Accompaniment Only) or SplitTrax CD.

Performance Time: ca. 45 Minutes

ISBN 9-781-4950-6089-2

EXCLUSIVELY DISTRIBUTED BY
HAL•LEONARD®
7777 W. BLUEMOUND RD. P.O. BOX 13819 MILWAUKEE, WI 53213

In Australia Contact:
Hal Leonard Australia Pty. Ltd.
4 Lentara Court
Cheltenham, Victoria, 3192 Australia
Email: ausadmin@halleonard.com.au

Visit Hal Leonard Online at
www.halleonard.com/church

Visit Shawnee Press Online at
www.shawneepress.com

58 Slower, more gracefully (♩ = ca. 112)

* Tune: THE HOLLY AND THE IVY, traditional English melody

INVITATION TO A MIRACLE - SAB

With stately dignity (♩ = ca. 108)

* Tune: TEMPUS ADEST FLORIDUM, *Piae Cantiones*, 1582

INVITATION TO A MIRACLE - SAB

8

157 **Quickly driving to the end** (♩ = ca. 120)

A PROCESSIONAL OF HOPE

Words by
JOSEPH M. MARTIN (BMI)
Quoting "O Come, O Come, Emmanuel"

Based on tunes:
VENI EMMANUEL
and **LEONI**
Arranged by
JOSEPH M. MARTIN

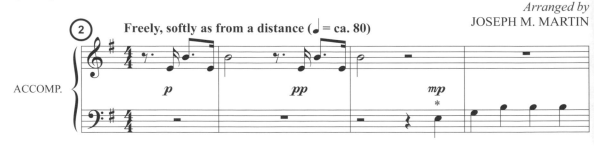

The choir may process, or a procession of candles may accompany the presentation of this opening piece. Acolytes may process in an orderly fashion, and illuminate the sanctuary as this brief introit is offered to establish the beginning of worship.

* Tune: VENI EMMANUEL, 15th century plainsong
** Measures 11-39 may be sung by 2 evenly divided unison SAB choirs, or by unison men and unison women.
† Tune: LEONI, traditional Hebrew melody

* Words: Latin Hymn; tr. John Mason Neale, 1818-1866
** Words: Joseph M. Martin

INVITATION TO A MIRACLE - SAB

prom - ise of re - demp - tion,__ and the__ dawn of

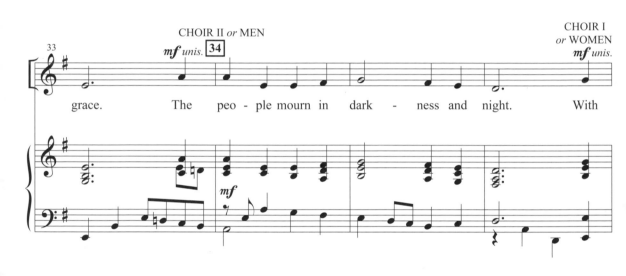

CHOIR II *or* **MEN**

CHOIR I
or **WOMEN**

grace. The peo - ple mourn in dark - ness and night. With

hope they wait the com - ing of the Light. * Re -

TUTTI

* Words: Latin Hymn; tr. John Mason Neale, 1818-1866

INVITATION TO A MIRACLE - SAB

NARRATOR 1

This is a season of miracles and wonders; a time to celebrate the glorious impossible of God's magnificent grace. Celebrate FAITH as God speaks His living Word into the darkness and awakens the world to His promise of grace. Hear this word from scripture:

NARRATOR 2

How beautiful on the mountains are the feet of those who bring good news, who proclaim peace, who bring good tidings, who proclaim salvation, who say to Zion, "Your God reigns!" Listen! Your watchmen lift up their voices; together they shout for joy. When the LORD returns to Zion, they will see it with their own eyes. Burst into songs of joy together, for the LORD has comforted His people, He has redeemed Jerusalem.

Isaiah 52:7-9 (adapted from NIV)*

JOY ARISING

Words by
JOSEPH M. MARTIN (BMI)

Based on tunes:
KINGS OF ORIENT
and **UKRAINIAN BELL CAROL**
Arranged by
JOSEPH M. MARTIN

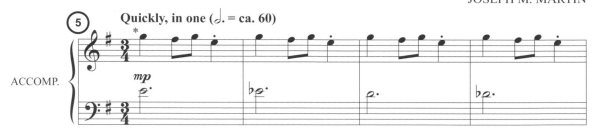

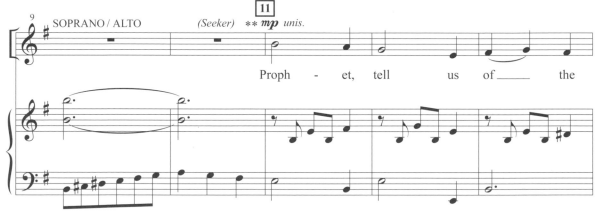

Proph - et, tell us of ____ the

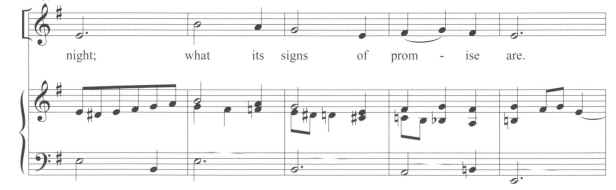

night; what its signs of prom - ise are.

* Tune: UKRAINIAN BELL CAROL, Mykola Leontovych, 1877-1921
** Tune: KINGS OF ORIENT, John Henry Hopkins, Jr., 1820-1891

20

22

Lift your voic - es in ju - bi - lant song to the Lord.

dim. poco a poco

p

Ha - va na - gi - la. Ha - va na - gi - la.

p

NARRATOR 1

This is a season of miracles and wonders; for God is stirring the souls of the people and sharing a new covenant of light to the people who walk in darkness. Celebrate HOPE as God's glory bursts into the darkness like a thousand stars of light. Hear the words of the prophet:

NARRATOR 2

Arise, shine, for your light has come, and the glory of the LORD rises upon you. See, darkness covers the earth and thick darkness is over the peoples, but the LORD rises upon you and His glory appears over you. Nations will come to your light, and kings to the brightness of your dawn.

Isaiah 60:1-3 (NIV)*

YOUR LIGHT HAS COME

Words and Music by
JON PAIGE (BMI)
and **JOSEPH M. MARTIN** (BMI)
Incorporating tune:
TEMPUS ADEST FLORIDUM

INVITATION TO A MIRACLE - SAB

30

32

a - tion. A - rise and shine; your__ Light has come. Let__

a - tion. Rise; your Light__ has__ come. Let__

joy a - wake the dawn. The glo -

joy a - wake the dawn. The glo -

- - ry__ of__ the__ Lord has come!

ry, glo - ry of the Lord has come!

34

Moun-tains ring and can - yons sing. Hear the proc - la - ma - tion.

Call His name Em - man - u - el: God with us a - bid - ing.

Now the heav - ens shine and tell. See His star is

38

NARRATOR 1

This is a season of miracles and wonders. Celebrate PEACE as God speaks to a young girl who embraces the Divine with gentle obedience. Listen to the words of this great announcement:

NARRATOR 2

God sent the angel Gabriel to Nazareth, a town in Galilee, to a virgin pledged to be married to a man named Joseph, a descendant of David. The virgin's name was Mary. The angel went to her and said, "Greetings, you who are highly favored! The Lord is with you." Mary was greatly troubled at his words and wondered what kind of greeting this might be. But the angel said to her, "Do not be afraid, Mary; you have found favor with God. You will conceive and give birth to a son, and you are to call Him Jesus. He will be great and will be called the Son of the Most High. The Lord God will give Him the throne of His father David, and He will reign over Jacob's descendants forever; His kingdom will never end."

Luke 1:26-33 (NIV) *

MY SOUL REJOICES IN THE LORD

Words by
JOSEPH M. MARTIN (BMI)
Quoting
"Come, Thou Long-Expected Jesus"

Music by
JOSEPH M. MARTIN
Incorporating tunes:
GREAT PHYSICIAN
and **HYFRYDOL**

INVITATION TO A MIRACLE - SAB

42

with us. Em - man - u - el, God is

with us. God is with us, Em-man-u-el.

Gently flowing (♩. = ca. 63)

SOPRANO SOLO

My

soul re - joic - es in the Lord. My heart ex - alts my Sav - ior;____

for He re - gards me with His love, and shows to me His

fa - vor.____ My soul re - joic - es in His light; and

I am filled with won - der.____ His grace speaks soft - ly

to the sky. Praise the name of Je - sus.

Come, Thou long - ex - pect - ed Je - sus, born to set___ Thy

19 *rit.*

81 Slower, freely ($\bullet. = $ ca. 46)

* *mp*

* Tune: HYFRYDOL, Rowland H. Prichard, 1811-1887
Words: Charles Wesley, 1707-1788

INVITATION TO A MIRACLE - SAB

NARRATOR 1

This is a season of miracles and wonders. God is speaking His LOVE in the world. Gather close, and gaze upon the manger of grace. See heaven's King choose a cradle of compassion rather than a throne of power. Jesus, the Savior, is born. Hear the timeless story:

NARRATOR 2

So Joseph also went up from the town of Nazareth in Galilee to Judea, to Bethlehem the town of David, because he belonged to the house and line of David. He went there to register with Mary, who was pledged to be married to him and was expecting a child. While they were there, the time came for the baby to be born, and she gave birth to her firstborn, a son. She wrapped Him in cloths and placed Him in a manger, because there was no guest room available for them.

Luke 2:4-7 (NIV)*

A CELTIC CRADLE CAROL

Words by
JOSEPH M. MARTIN (BMI)
Quoting
"Love Divine, All Loves Excelling"

Tune: **SUO GÂN**
Traditional Welsh Lullaby
Arranged by
JOSEPH M. MARTIN

60

far from dan-ger, shep - herds guard on bend - ed knees.

In the si-lence, Love is sleep-ing; no more weep-ing,

SOLO
mp

S. *p*
A.
Oo
B. *p*

Joy of heav'n to earth come down.

Joy of heav'n to earth come down.

* Words: Charles Wesley, 1707-1788

INVITATION TO A MIRACLE - SAB

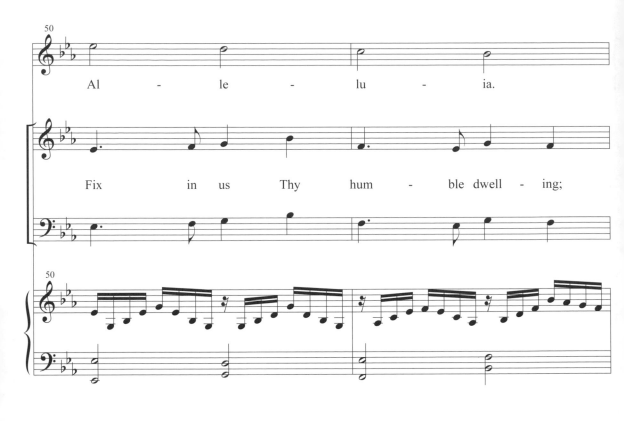

all com-pas - sion. Pure, un-bound-ed love Thou art.

Vis - it us with Thy sal - va - tion.

En - ter ev - 'ry trem - bling heart.

NARRATOR 1

This is a season of miracles and wonders. Even the heavens are declaring the birth of Jesus. Celebrate JOY as the Judean hillsides echo with the voices of angels proclaiming good tidings to simple shepherds. Hear this account from scripture:

NARRATOR 2

And there were shepherds living out in the fields nearby, keeping watch over their flocks at night. An angel of the Lord appeared to them, and the glory of the Lord shone around them, and they were terrified. But the angel said to them, "Do not be afraid. I bring you good news that will cause great joy for all the people. Today in the town of David a Savior has been born to you; He is the Messiah, the Lord. This will be a sign to you: You will find a baby wrapped in cloths and lying in a manger."

Suddenly a great company of the heavenly host appeared with the angel, praising God and saying, "Glory to God in the highest heaven, and on earth peace to those on whom His favor rests."

Luke 2:8-14 (NIV) *

ALLELUIA! CHRIST IS BORN!

Words and Music by
JOSEPH M. MARTIN (BMI)
Incorporating tune:
SICILIAN MARINERS
Traditional Sicilian Melody

The bells of heav-en are ring-ing. They ring a ju-bi-lant song.

The an-gels join with_ sing-ing. They bring a song to the Lord; to the

INVITATION TO A MIRACLE - SAB

72

* Tune: SICILIAN MARINERS, Traditional Sicilian Melody
The European Magazine and Review, 1792

INVITATION TO A MIRACLE - SAB

un - to us a___ Son is giv'n.

mp *mf*
An - gels now are wing - ing; joy - ful ti - dings bring - ing.

f
Ju - bi - la - te, ju - bi - la - te. Christ___ is___ born!

and bring a song to the Lord; to the Son who was born. Al - le -

end of __ sad - ness. Bring to the Son who was born. Al - le -

lu - ia. Sing al - le - lu - ia. Break forth in

lu - ia. Sing al - le - lu - ia. Break forth in

ju - bi - lant song. __ Come raise a glad al - le - lu - ia.

NARRATOR 1

This is a season of miracles and wonders. God is drawing the world to His grace. His light goes before us, and we would follow. Celebrate LIGHT as a sacred star shines silver promise on golden sand. Walk with the dreamers and seekers to a place of devotion and worship. Hear these words that changed the world:

NARRATOR 2

In the beginning was the Word, and the Word was with God, and the Word was God. He was with God in the beginning. Through Him all things were made; without Him nothing was made that has been made. In Him was life, and that life was the light of all mankind. The light shines in the darkness, and the darkness has not overcome it.

The true light that gives light to everyone was coming into the world. He was in the world, and though the world was made through Him, the world did not recognize Him. He came to that which was His own, but His own did not receive Him. Yet to all who did receive Him, to those who believed in His name, He gave the right to become children of God.

*John 1:1-5, 9-12 (NIV)**

WOULD I MISS THE MIRACLE?

Words by
PAMELA STEWART (BMI)

Music by
DOUGLAS NOLAN (BMI)
and JOSEPH M. MARTIN (BMI)

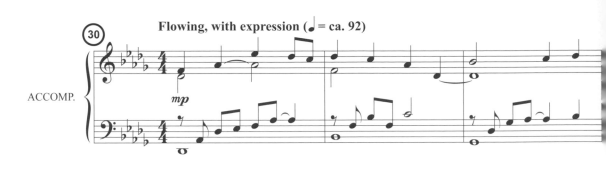

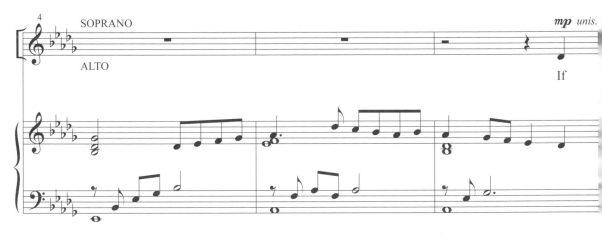

an - gels filled the skies to - night, would I hear them

sing? Would to - mor - row find me say - ing

it was all a dream?

BARITONE

Would I leave my

bed and go out - side to hear their song?

mir - a - cle? Would I see the King?

If a

stran - ger knocked up - on my door to - night in deep - est

NARRATOR 1

This is a season of miracles and wonders. Celebrate LIFE and walk the path of service. God has begun a great new work among us. Humble your hearts with thanksgiving, worship and prayer. Bow, bend, and become. Take the miracle within you, and let its light shine from the windows of your heart. Let the darkness see and believe. Let the shadows surrender to light. Let the miracle begin! Come celebrate Jesus! Know the wonder of grace!

A GLORIA GATHERING

Arranged by
JOSEPH M. MARTIN (BMI)

Based on carols:
"Angels, from the Realms of Glory"
"Angels We Have Heard on High"
"Sing We Now of Christmas"
"O Come, All Ye Faithful"
"Hark! the Herald Angels Sing"

Moderately fast, with growing excitement (♩ = ca. 120)

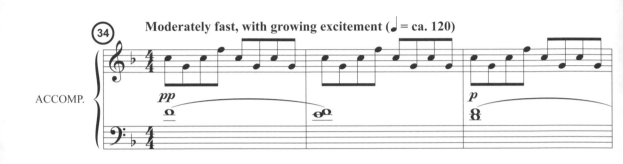

INVITATION TO A MIRACLE - SAB

* Tune: REGENT SQUARE, Henry T. Smart, 1813-1879
Words: James Montgomery, 1771-1854

King!

An - gels we have heard on high,

sweet - ly sing - ing o'er the plains, and the moun - tains

* Tune: GLORIA, traditional French melody
Words: traditional French carol

INVITATION TO A MIRACLE - SAB

Sing we now of Christ - mas.

pa, pa, pa, pa, pa, pa, pa, pa,

pa, pa, pa, pa, pa, pa, pa, pa,

Sing we__ all No - el! Sing we now of

pa, pa, pa, pa, pa, pa, pa, pa, pa,

pa, pa, pa, pa, pa, pa, pa, pa, pa,

* Tune: NOËL NOUVELET, traditional French melody
Words: traditional French carol

INVITATION TO A MIRACLE - SAB

* Tune: ADESTE FIDELES, John Francis Wade, 1711-1786
Words: Latin hymn, ascribed to John Francis Wade, 1711-1786

INVITATION TO A MIRACLE - SAB

Join the tri - umph of the skies.___ With th'an - gel - ic

host pro - claim, "Christ is___ born in Beth - le - hem!"

Hark! the her - ald an - gels sing, "Glo - ry___ to the

new - born King!"

INVITATION TO A MIRACLE - SAB

high - est! Sing glo - ry to God in the high - est!

Christ, the Lord, is born! Christ is born! Christ is

born! Christ is born!

110 The publisher hereby grants permission to reprint the material within the box for the purpose of making performance of this cantata possible with congregational participation, provided that a sufficient quantity of copies of the entire cantata has been purchased for performance by the choir and accompanist. The music must be reproduced with the title and all credits including the copyright notice.

HARK! THE HERALD ANGELS SING

Words by
CHARLES WESLEY (1707-1788)

Tune: **MENDELSSOHN**
by FELIX MENDELSSOHN (1809-1847)
Arranged by
JOSEPH M. MARTIN (BMI)